Lil' Sass and The Adventure of Sadness

Written by Christie Mann

Lil' Sass Explores her Emotions and Learns that it's OK to Express Sadness

Dedication & Acknowledgements

For all the little hearts in my life, watching you grow is one of my greatest joys, and it inspired me to write this series. And for your mothers and fathers—because without them, you would not be here and Sass would not have been birthed.
Thank you!

For my healers, teachers and tribe. Sass was born from these classrooms and teachings and she is a portal through which I can spread these technologies and teachings. Ho! And So, it is!
Sat Nam!

For my Momma, I see you and I love you. Cape On!

For all of us who, at times, might be afraid to feel and express our emotions but move past the fear to allow ourselves to have the full range of our human experience.

Last, but not least, for the real Mrs. Moo: You may truly never know just how significant the positive impact your true friendship has had on my family and me. Thank you for letting me sit at your kitchen table and feel my emotions.
I love you.

Cape On!

A Note to Parents and Caretakers:

I'm super excited for you and your kid(s) to meet Lil' Sass and accompany her on her adventures as she learns about her emotions. This topic of both having and being with our emotions isn't always an easy one. I learned this through my own journey, which is why I wanted to create Lil' Sass: to help adults and children talk about and experience emotions in a healthy, supportive way. I hope these stories support you as much as they support your child(ren). I share this with you with deep gratitude and respect for your dedication to your role as a parent and caretaker.

Cape On!

Sincerely,

Christie Mann

Meet Lil' Sass.

She is ten years old and is independent, clever, and determined. Her real name is Grace, but ever since she was a baby, her parents have called her Lil' Sass because she is just so adventurous and curious.

Lil' Sass lives in Venice Beach, California with her Mom. She likes roller-skating, going on adventures, and making new friends. Her dad used to live with them, but he and Mom started arguing a lot, and then he left. A few days after he left, her friend, Mrs. Moo, gave her The Red Cape.

Mrs. Moo is a kind and wise older lady who rents the little house in the backyard. Her job is to help people feel things. When she gave Lil' Sass The Red Cape, she said, "Sass, you can go inside of this Cape and feel whatever you are feeling. Just say, 'Cape On!' There, inside your Cape, you can explore and express all of your emotions."

"Feeling is a gift you give yourself. It is your right as a human being to experience your emotions— all of them." Emotion is the word Mrs. Moo uses to describe feelings like anger, sadness, and joy. As Sass goes about her adventures, she explores new emotions with her Cape.

The Adventure of Sadness

Lil' Sass could not sleep, so she decided to create an adventure in her imagination instead. She imagined that she and Tommy had roller skates with rockets on them. Together, they flew around the roller rink. Then, she imagined the rockets on their skates breaking, and she imagined herself crashing down to the ground. This was a scary thought, and it did not feel good.

Sass heard a muffled sound, so she put her ear against the bedroom wall. On the other side, she could hear her mom crying. Uh-oh, it sounds like Mom's rockets have broken and she is crashing too, Sass thought. Ever since Dad went away, Mom had been so busy and so sad. Sass hugged The Red Cape.

It felt soft and comforting around her. She also noticed that her tummy felt as tight as a knot. Then, she felt the knot move up into her throat, and Sass began to cry. She knew this emotion. This was sadness. There in bed, Lil' Sass cried and thought about all the things people had told her about sadness.

There was the time when a babysitter came to take care of her when Mom and Dad went on a trip. Lil' Sass cried and cried as her parents drove away. She was so sad because she did not want them to go, and she was afraid they would not come back.

Her babysitter said, "Stop crying, Sass. Big girls and good little girls don't cry." Sass wanted to be a big girl, or at least a good little girl, so she stopped crying.

Then there was the time when Frankie and Sarah said they did not want to play with her anymore. Lil' Sass started crying and Frankie said; "Stop crying! Crying is for babies, and besides, you look ugly when you cry."

Sass did not want to be a baby, and she did not want to be ugly, so she stopped crying.

Especially after Dad left, she felt so much sadness. She could tell that Mom did, too. The first day she woke up without him, she hugged Mom and started to cry. Mom said, "Oh Sass, please do not cry. It makes me sad to see you sad. We need to be strong right now."

Sass did not want to upset Mom, because Mom was already upset. She wanted to be strong, so she stopped crying—but she still could not stop feeling sad.

Lil' Sass thought about what her babysitter, Frankie and Mom had said to her about being sad. She listened to her mother crying in the next room.

Sass felt sad because her mom was sad and because her dad was not there.
"Why is it so bad to be sad and show it?" she asked the moon. Then she thought about Mrs. Moo and The Red Cape.

When she gave Lil' Sass the cape, Mrs. Moo said, "Sass, sometimes you will be so sad that you will feel like you could cry and cry and cry. That is okay. Use your Red Cape to let the sadness pour right out of you. Let the sadness take over your whole body. You can even shake with tears if you want. That is okay. Let yourself do that!

Do not ever think it is wrong to be sad or to cry. Feeling this emotion is your right as a human being."

At the time, Sass did not really understand
what Mrs. Moo was talking about,
but now it was all making sense.
Letting herself feel her sadness was
a gift she gave herself!
Sass tied her cape around her
neck and said, "Cape On!"
Then she had a big, long cry.
She cried hard and soft,
and then she made big noises and little
noises. She let her body shake until
her tears made a puddle on her floor.

After some time, the crying slowed down. Lil' Sass noticed that the knots in her belly and throat were gone. Then, she began to realize that she was not feeling so sad anymore. She felt very tired, but she also felt much better.

Sass thought about all the things people had said to her about sadness. Now that she had let herself feel sad and have a good cry, she now knew that some of those things were not the same as what she was learning. It was not true that big kids and good little kids did not cry.

Baby!

"Of course they do," she said out loud. "I'm a GOOD kid and I cry! I'm actually stronger because I feel sad sometimes." She looked at herself in the mirror and said, "And I look beautiful when I cry!"

Then she thought about how Mom had asked her to "be strong and not cry."
Sass realized that her mom must think she has to "be strong and not cry" for Sass.

Sass blew a kiss through the bedroom wall.
She thought about how lucky she was to have
the Red Cape, because she was learning a lot
about her feelings and emotions. Sass thought
that maybe she needed to make a Red Cape
for her Mom, so that her Mom could know
that feeling her sadness was her right
as a human being, too.

With that, Sass got out of bed and snuck to her Mom's door.

She quietly opened it, and tiptoed to the side of her mom's bed to lay the Red Cape over the blankets. She put her little face right up to her Mom's face and whispered, "Mom, you look beautiful when you cry, too.

Cape On!"

Mom woke up with tears in her eyes. She put her hands around Sass' face and said, "Thank you for sharing your special cape with me, Sass. Cape On!" Lil' Sass' mom pulled her up into the bed with her, and they snuggled and cried together until they both fell back to sleep.

The next morning, Sass and her mom cuddled in bed. Mom said, "Sass, it is true: we all have emotions. Having emotions is normal, and we should all be allowed to express them and feel them when they come. I am very proud of you for using your Cape to explore your emotions."

Sass said, "Thanks Mom, I am having fun on my adventures. Let's make you your very own Cape, so you can have your own adventures, too!" Sass' mom agreed, and the two of them set out on an adventure to find all the supplies for her mom's new Cape.

On their way out the door, Lil' Sass saw herself in the mirror again. She realized she looked joyful! She smiled as she said to her reflection, "'Cape On!' is catching on!"

Discussion Guide

Cape On, Moms, Dads and Caretakers!

Lil' Sass is here to teach your kids about feeling their emotions all the way, and empowering them to do so with confidence. But she can't do it alone! As you read through Sass' adventures, please use the following questions to stimulate discussions with your kids about their emotions and their relationship with their emotions.

I encourage you to be open by revealing some of the toughest emotions you've experienced in a way that your kids can understand. Then invite them to do the same, and be ready to hold space and support whatever comes up for them.

Feeling and experiencing our emotions is a lifelong journey, and together, we can help point kids along the way. Remember what Mrs. Moo says, "Feeling emotions is our right as human beings!"

Cape On!

Questions:

- What are some of the toughest emotions you've felt?
  How did you handle them?

- Have you ever seen me feel sad? Your friends? Your siblings?
  Other grown-ups?

- Sass feels really sad about her dad being gone.
  What are some things that make you feel sad?

- Sass gets a knot in her stomach and throat when she is sad.
  What happens in your body?

- What have you done in the past when you've
  felt sad?

- What could you do the next
  time you feel sad?

- What are you learning about
  emotions?

- What other emotions are you
  curious about?

READY TO CAPE ON?

Visit the Sass Shop to get a cape
for Mom, Dad, caretakers and kiddos!

FREE BONUSES!

Discover free bonuses for Lil' Sass readers!
Visit www.lilsass.com

EXPLORE MORE BOOKS
by Christie Mann

#CAPEON

About the Author

Christie Mann has made it her mission to be an 'ever-student' to fulfill her purpose of being a leader who develops leaders, who develop leaders. Christie is an author, spiritual psychologist, leadership coach, learning consultant, trainer, speaker and Kundalini Yoga & Meditation teacher who designs and facilitates transformational content and experiences that make our world a happier, healthier and more connected place to be.

At 13-years-old, Christie's life suddenly and dramatically shifted when she suffered some devastating losses and was thrust into a leadership position, which subsequently, impacted her relationship with her own emotional growth. She has spent the better part of the past two decades on her own corrective path and, because of this, has a sincere desire to encourage others to have a healthier and more responsible relationship with their emotions.

She is the creator of The Adventures of Lil' Sass, a series of personal development books for young people, accompanied by supporting accessories & experiences - a brand that teaches the importance and value of being with our own emotions and shows us how much JOY we can experience when we allow ourselves to be fully self-expressed. She draws inspiration for the characters, stories and accessories from her own life experiences and her learnings from Therapy, the Co-Active methodology through CTI, a Master's Degree in the Practices and Principles of Spiritual Psychology from the University of Santa Monica, and her practice of the ancient technology of Kundalini Yoga. Christie also obtained an Undergraduate-Degree in Media, Information and Technoculture from the University of Western Ontario.

Originally from a small town in Ontario, Canada, Christie now lives in Venice Beach, California where you can find her at the Venice Roller Rink, the sunny shores of the Santa Monica Pier or at RAMA, a local Kundalini Yoga studio. An Auntie many times over, she's in awe of children's resilience and emotional flexibility and champions adults' rights to have and express emotions too.

Cape On!

A Deeper Cut on the Dedication & Acknowledgements

For all the little hearts in my life: Carson, Mia, Kingston, Cee Cee, Abbey, Will, Sebby, Hugo, Willow, Tommy, Jake, Lily, Brooks, Biba, Ma'ila, Rafi, Benji, Ellis, Althea, Alec, Mavis, Véronique, Freddy, Camille, Nik, Oliver, Luke, Gen, Gabby, Sophia, Reese, Tessa, Chloe, Mila, Jamie, Nathan, Noora & Israa. Watching you grow is one of my greatest joys, and it inspired me to write this series and create this brand. And for your mothers and fathers – because without them you would not be here and neither would Sass. And for D, for reigniting the spark of Sass in me – so she could be birthed.

Thank you to my dear friends, whom I call family. And to my dear family, whom I call friends.

For my healers, teachers and tribe. For Katherine Belfontaine for being the first one to make it safe to express my emotions—all of them. For Henry, Karen and Laura for birthing CTI/Co-Active and my Co-Active Family for creating experiences and circles where I am safe to go deeper and share more of my authentic self. For John: Thank you for your grace, equanimity and unconditional love. For my Purple Hearts, Teachers Ron and Mary Hulnick, and the practices and principles of Spiritual Psychology from USM. For Pam, thank you for helping me heal my body and introducing me to Melinda to heal on other planes. For Birch, you are a goddess and a magician. For Britta and Lee Eskey and the deep healing and courageous expression of ALL emotions through the COR experiences and brave community. For my community of Yogis and Teachers: Hawijian, Tej, Guru Jagat, Gurujas, Jai Gopal, Raghubir and the study and practice of Kundalini Yoga. Sass was born from these classrooms and she is a portal through which I can spread these technologies and teachings. Ho! And So, it is! Sat Nam!

For Pops, Momma and Stuy, I see you and I love you. Cape On!

For all of us who at times might be afraid to feel and express our emotions but, regardless, move past the fear to allow ourselves to truly have the full range of our human experience.

Last, but not least, for the real Mrs. Moo: You may truly never know just how significant the positive impact your true friendship has had on me and my family. Thank you for letting me sit at your kitchen table and feel my emotions. I love you.

Cape On!

CPSIA information can be obtained
at www.ICGtesting.com
Printed in the USA
BVHW06s2255040918
R9030200001B/R90302PG525872BVX2B/1/P